AI-Driven Marketing for Small Businesses

The Proven Blueprint to Automate, Personalize, and Scale Your Marketing Smarter

Written by
Eric LeBouthillier

AcraSolution | 2025 1st Edition
www.acrasolution.com

Preface

Why This Book Exists

Marketing used to be a guessing game. Small businesses would throw money at ads or social posts — hoping something would work. But those days are over.

AI has changed the rules.
It's no longer just for big brands. Today, AI is the smartest, most affordable marketing assistant a small business can have — working 24/7, learning as it goes.

The problem?
Most SMBs don't know where to start.

This book is your roadmap.
Whether you're a solopreneur or a growing team, you'll learn exactly how to use AI tools to generate leads, boost sales, and free up your time — without needing to be tech-savvy.

Each chapter is:

- **Simple**, not full of jargon
- **Actionable**, with real tools and examples
- **Focused on growth**, not theory

I wrote this book because small businesses deserve more than trial and error. You deserve smart marketing that works.

Let's make that happen — together.

— ***Eric LeBouthillier***
Author & Cybersecurity Strategist

For permission requests or inquiries, contact the publisher through the website : www.acrasolution.com

LEGAL DISCLAIMER

This eBook is provided for informational purposes only and does not constitute legal, financial, or professional advice. The author and publisher have made every reasonable effort to ensure the accuracy and completeness of the information contained herein; however, neither assumes any responsibility for errors, omissions, or contrary interpretations of the subject matter.

Readers are encouraged to consult with qualified professionals for specific advice tailored to their individual needs. The mention of any products, services, or third-party entities does not imply an endorsement or guarantee of their effectiveness or suitability. Any application of the strategies and recommendations presented is at the reader's discretion and risk.

The author and publisher shall not be liable for any damages (including, without limitation, direct, indirect, incidental, or consequential) caused by the use, misuse, or interpretation of the information herein. All references to regulatory standards, statutes, or compliance requirements are informational and do not replace official legal counsel.

By reading and applying the concepts in this eBook, you acknowledge that you bear sole responsibility for the outcomes of your decisions and actions. If you do not agree to these terms, please discontinue use of this publication immediately.

Table of Contents

Chapter 1: The Marketing Revolution — Why AI Matters Now

Introduction

Marketing has always been the heartbeat of business growth — but for small and mid-sized businesses (SMBs), it's often a game of limitations. Limited time. Limited staff. Limited budget. Meanwhile, larger brands flood the market with ads, dominate search results, and run complex data-driven campaigns that feel out of reach for everyone else.

Until now.

Artificial intelligence (AI) has changed the rules. Not just for marketers, but for every business that wants to grow smarter, faster, and with more precision. AI isn't just another tool in the toolbox — it's the engine that powers an entirely new way of connecting with customers.

For the first time, SMBs can compete — and even outperform — bigger competitors by using AI to automate what used to be manual, personalize what used to be generic, and predict what used to be guesswork.

In this chapter, we'll explore what AI in marketing *really* means, why this shift is so transformative, and how small businesses are using it right now to increase visibility, drive growth, and scale like never before.

What Is AI in Marketing (Real Definition, Not Hype)

Let's cut through the noise.

When most people hear "AI in marketing," they picture chatbots and robotic-sounding emails. Or worse — they assume it's only for tech giants with endless budgets. But in real, practical terms, **AI in marketing simply means using software that learns from data to make better, faster marketing decisions.**

Here's a breakdown in plain English:

- **AI detects patterns** — in customer behavior, website activity, purchase history, or social media engagement.
- **It uses those patterns to predict outcomes** — such as which leads are likely to convert or which content will perform best.
- **It takes action at scale** — automating personalized messages, ad placements, content delivery, and more.

This turns chaotic marketing into intelligent, responsive systems that work 24/7 — no extra team required.

You don't need to be technical to use AI. You just need to know where it adds value.

Core Capabilities of AI Marketing Tools

- **Segmentation**: Automatically group customers based on behavior, not assumptions
- **Personalization**: Deliver emails, web content, or offers tailored to individual preferences
- **Forecasting**: Predict which products or services a customer is likely to buy next
- **Automation**: Schedule and optimize campaigns across channels without manual input

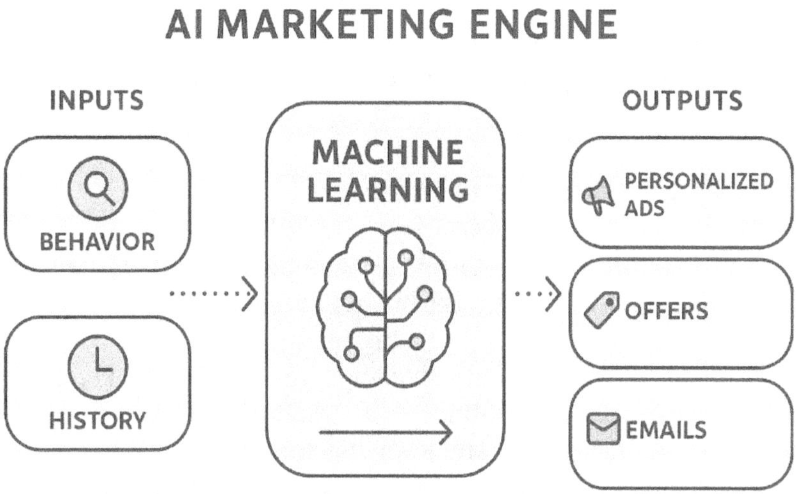

Bottom line: AI doesn't replace marketers — it empowers them. For SMBs, that means finally having the same intelligence and efficiency as big brands, without the complexity.

Why Small Businesses Can Now Compete with Big Brands

For decades, larger businesses held all the marketing power. They had access to market research teams, high-end CRM platforms, media buying agencies, and more. Small businesses, on the other hand, were forced to rely on intuition, word of mouth, or painfully slow trial-and-error.

But AI shifts that balance.

Today, the same AI tools that Fortune 500s use are available to SMBs — often in affordable, plug-and-play formats. These tools don't require a data scientist or an agency retainer. Many are built specifically for SMB use, with pre-trained models and user-friendly dashboards.

Here's what this means in practice:

- **Affordable Reach**: AI-powered ad platforms like Meta Ads and Google Ads optimize budget in real time — so your $100 can work as hard as a big brand's $10,000.
- **Speed to Market**: Launch campaigns in hours, not weeks. AI can generate headlines, test variations, and adjust targeting faster than any human team.
- **Data Access**: Even without a research department, AI tools can analyze your website traffic, email clicks, and sales data to surface clear insights.
- **Customer Intelligence**: Tools like HubSpot, ActiveCampaign, and Klaviyo use AI to score leads, recommend send times, and trigger automations — all based on behavior.

Tactical Best Practices

- Use AI-based CRM platforms to automate lead nurturing
- Run dynamic Facebook or Google ads that adjust automatically to top-performing content
- Deploy AI-driven email subject lines to increase open rates
- Use smart chatbots to qualify leads and reduce support load

The playing field has officially been leveled — not by budgets, but by intelligence.

The Shift from Guesswork to Precision

Marketing used to be all about hunches. You'd create a campaign, send it out into the world, and hope it worked. If it didn't, you'd try again with something slightly different — often without understanding why it failed in the first place.

AI makes marketing scientific.

Today, every click, view, scroll, and purchase feeds into models that learn what works and what doesn't — instantly. The guesswork is gone. You no longer have to wonder which subject line will perform better or which audience segment is most engaged. AI will tell you.

Precision Marketing in Action

- **Content Optimization**: AI tools like Jasper or Copy.ai can write and A/B test dozens of ad variations or blog headlines.
- **Smart Timing**: Platforms like Mailchimp use AI to send emails when each recipient is most likely to open.
- **Behavior-Based Offers**: Your website can display different offers to first-time vs. returning visitors.
- **Lead Scoring**: AI evaluates lead quality based on real-time behavior and recommends sales follow-ups accordingly.

Checklist: Signs You're Still in Guesswork Mode

- You send the same newsletter to your entire email list
- You create ads without A/B testing multiple versions
- You base campaigns on gut feeling rather than user data
- You don't know which channel gives you the highest ROI

If any of these ring true, AI can help you move from blind effort to guided execution.

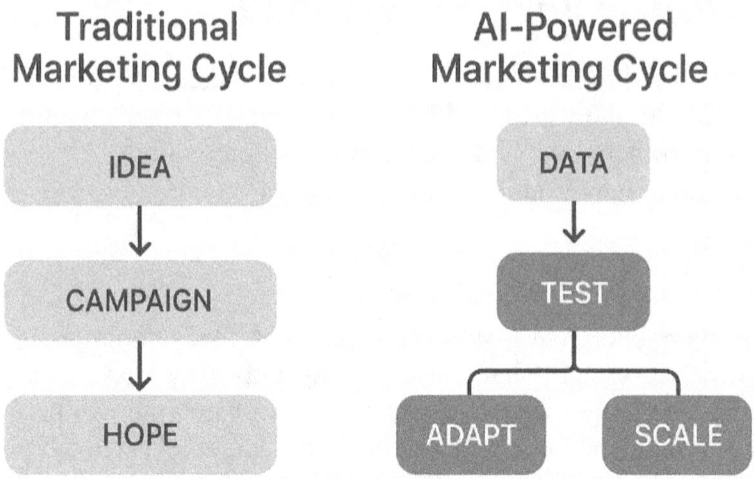

Real-World Example: Traditional vs AI-Driven Campaign

Business: Regional Home Cleaning Company
Challenge: Low ad performance and high customer churn
Traditional Approach:

- Static Facebook ads targeting all adults within a 25-mile radius
- Same landing page and messaging for everyone
- 1.5% conversion rate, no clarity on what was or wasn't working

AI-Driven Approach:

- Installed AI-based analytics on their website to track behavior
- Used customer data to create three key segments: young professionals, busy parents, and senior homeowners
- Ran tailored ads and landing pages for each segment
- Used AI to A/B test and refine headlines and visuals
- Conversion rate jumped to 6.8%
- Customer retention increased due to more relevant messaging

What Went Right

- Micro-targeting based on behavior, not assumptions
- Personalized content and offers for each audience
- Continuous optimization through AI feedback loops

Key Takeaway

Even without a full marketing team, the business scaled faster and more efficiently — using the same data and budget, but far more strategically.

Common Pitfalls to Avoid

- **Over-Automation**: Letting AI handle everything without human oversight leads to tone-deaf or irrelevant content.
- **One-Size-Fits-All Tools**: Choose platforms designed for your size and industry — not just the most popular.
- **Neglecting Data Quality**: AI is only as good as the data you feed it. Inaccurate or outdated inputs lead to poor decisions.
- **Thinking AI = Set and Forget**: The best results come when AI is paired with human creativity and judgment.

Conclusion

AI isn't the future of marketing — it's the *now*. For SMBs, it offers a rare and powerful chance to play on equal footing with industry giants. With the right tools and a clear strategy, you can stop guessing and start growing.

The real opportunity lies not just in using AI, but in using it *intelligently*. To know your customers better. To make every dollar go further. And to turn data into decisions — fast.

Next Steps

Take inventory of your current marketing activities. Which ones feel repetitive, vague, or inconsistent? Those are the perfect entry points for AI.

In **Chapter 2: Know Your Audience — Using AI for Customer Insights**, we'll dive into how AI helps you truly understand your audience — not just demographically, but behaviorally. You'll learn how to use AI-powered tools to uncover what your customers want, when they want it, and how to deliver messaging that resonates on a personal level.

Chapter 2: Know Your Audience — Using AI for Customer Insights

Introduction

Every successful marketing strategy starts with one critical truth: **know your audience, or risk being ignored**. For SMBs, this has historically been a challenge. Limited budgets and time meant relying on assumptions, anecdotal feedback, or outdated surveys to understand who customers really are. And when messaging misses the mark, so does growth.

AI flips the script. It allows businesses of any size to go beyond surface-level demographics and tap directly into *real customer behavior*. With the right tools, you can now observe how people interact with your brand in real time, understand what motivates them, and even predict what they'll want next — all without needing a data team.

This chapter dives into how SMBs can harness AI to unlock powerful customer insights, build more effective personas, anticipate buyer needs, and tailor every offer with unmatched precision.

Tools to Discover Audience Behavior

Knowing your audience starts with seeing how they actually behave — not just what they say. AI-powered tools now make it possible to track, analyze, and interpret this behavior at scale.

Key Tools and What They Do

- **Chatbots** (e.g., Drift, Intercom): Capture customer questions, hesitations, and intent in real time. These conversations reveal friction points and buying signals.
- **Website Analytics** (e.g., Hotjar, Microsoft Clarity): Heatmaps and session recordings show what users click, scroll, and ignore on your site — giving insight into interest and confusion.
- **CRM Platforms with AI** (e.g., HubSpot, Zoho CRM): Automatically score leads and identify which behaviors correlate with purchases or churn.
- **Social Listening Tools** (e.g., Brand24, Sprout Social): Monitor how customers talk about your brand and industry across channels, using sentiment analysis to understand tone.

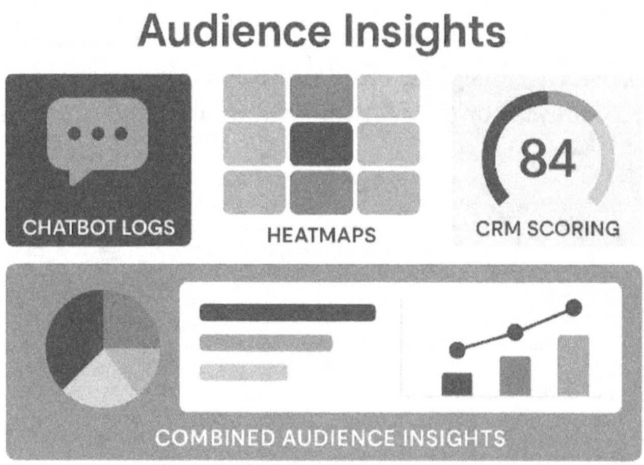

Tactical Benefits for SMBs

- Discover which pages or products are most engaging (and which aren't)
- Identify the drop-off points in your customer journey
- Understand which questions customers ask before converting
- See how different audience segments behave across channels

AI for Persona Development

Creating marketing personas used to be an exercise in creativity: inventing fictional customers based on assumptions and basic demographic data. But AI makes it possible to **build real personas from real behavior** — and continuously refine them as data evolves.

How AI Builds Smarter Personas

- **Clustering Algorithms**: AI groups users based on behavior, preferences, and purchase history to reveal natural customer segments.
- **Natural Language Processing (NLP)**: Analyzes survey responses, support tickets, or chatbot transcripts to extract common language and sentiment.
- **Predictive Scoring**: Assigns likelihoods to different personas based on how they respond to content, emails, or offers.

Real-World SMB Persona Example

A boutique fitness studio used AI tools to analyze booking behavior and email engagement. The system identified three core personas:

1. **The Busy Professional** – Books evening classes, responds to schedule-focused messaging
2. **The Social Exerciser** – Shares content online, refers friends, attends group classes
3. **The Results Seeker** – Reads nutrition blogs, opens transformation emails, prefers 1-on-1 coaching

Armed with this insight, the studio tailored offers, class reminders, and content to each group — boosting engagement and retention.

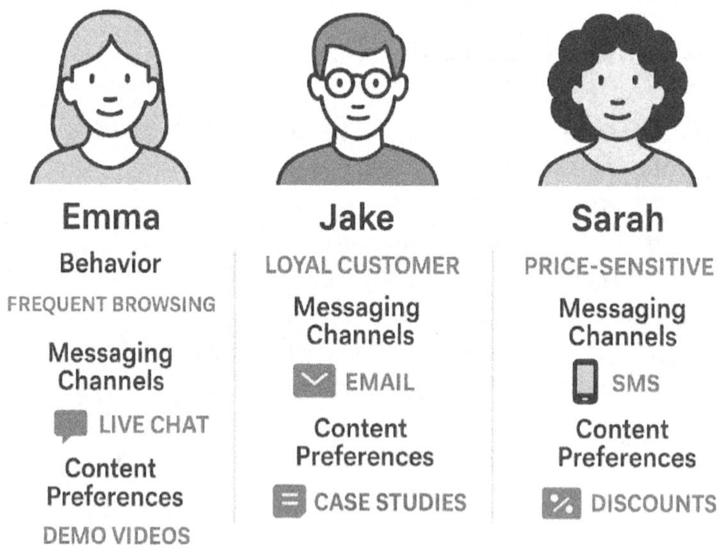

Predicting Customer Needs with AI

Knowing who your customers are is one thing. Predicting what they'll want next — that's the power of AI at its best.

AI can analyze thousands of data points to detect subtle patterns humans might miss. These models then make accurate predictions about behavior, needs, or timing — helping you reach customers with the right message before they even ask.

Examples of Predictive Insight in Action

- **Purchase Timing**: AI can flag when a customer is likely to reorder or upgrade — and trigger a campaign automatically.
- **Churn Prediction**: If engagement drops below a threshold, AI can recommend win-back strategies or offers.
- **Next-Best Product**: Based on browsing or past purchases, AI suggests cross-sells that feel helpful, not pushy.
- **Content Preferences**: AI tracks which blogs, videos, or emails each segment engages with — helping you serve content they actually care about.

Checklist: How to Start Using Predictive AI

- Connect your CRM and email platform to a tool that supports predictive scoring
- Use AI heatmaps or journey tracking to flag behavior changes
- Automate campaign triggers based on key signals (e.g., cart abandonment, support ticket closed, 30-day inactivity)

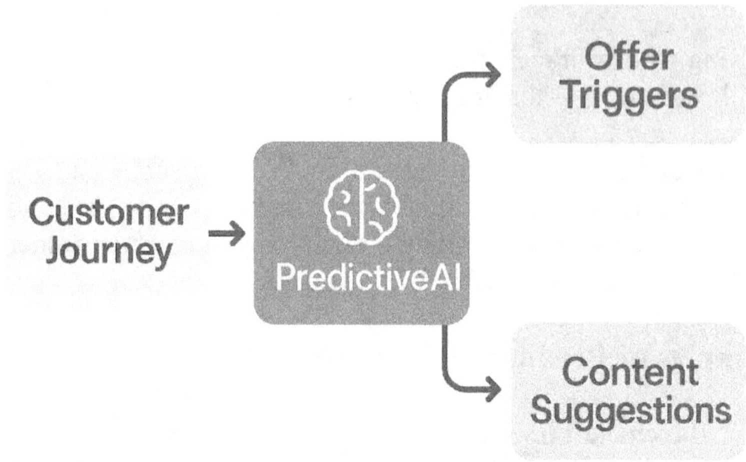

How to Tailor Offers and Language for Impact

Once you know who your customers are — and what they need — the final step is personalization: making sure the *right message* reaches the *right person* at the *right time*.

AI allows you to do this not just at the campaign level, but at the individual level — even if you're working with a small team.

Personalization Powered by AI

- **Email Content**: AI tools like Persado or Phrasee write subject lines and copy that adapt to user preferences.
- **Landing Pages**: Platforms like Unbounce can dynamically change text, images, or calls-to-action based on visitor data.
- **Ad Creative**: Meta Ads and Google Ads use AI to serve the highest-performing variations to the right segments.
- **Website Chatbots**: Greet users with different questions or offers based on referral source or past behavior.

Tactical Best Practices

- Create segmented content libraries for different personas
- Let AI tools test and adjust your messaging based on live performance
- Always collect and tag behavioral data — it powers everything else
- Avoid one-size-fits-all emails; instead, automate sequences for different journeys

---

Real-World Example: Understanding Customers with AI

Business Type: Online Specialty Tea Retailer
Challenge: Low customer retention and stagnant conversion rates
Old Approach: Sent the same newsletter to all customers with seasonal promotions and product highlights

AI-Enhanced Approach:

- Installed an AI-based analytics tool that tracked purchase and browsing behavior
- Identified distinct customer clusters: gift buyers, wellness seekers, and flavor explorers
- Tailored product suggestions, bundles, and emails based on segment behavior
- Implemented predictive timing to send re-engagement offers just before customers typically dropped off

Results:

- Email open rates increased 36%
- Repeat purchase rate doubled
- Bounce rate on site dropped by 22%

What We Learn

When messaging matches intent — and timing matches behavior — results follow. This wasn't a redesign or a rebrand. It was simply knowing their customers better and using AI to act on that knowledge.

Common Pitfalls to Avoid

- **Over-segmentation**: Too many micro-audiences can overcomplicate your messaging — aim for clarity over complexity
- **Ignoring Negative Signals**: What customers *don't* do (abandon carts, skip emails) is just as valuable as what they *do*

- **Failing to Act on Insights**: Data without follow-through wastes time — every insight should drive a real action
- **Relying Solely on Demographics**: Age and location are only part of the story — behavior and context matter more

Conclusion

Understanding your audience has always been the cornerstone of effective marketing — but AI now makes it easier, deeper, and faster than ever. Whether you're just starting out or scaling an established brand, AI-powered customer insights give you the clarity to speak to your market with relevance, precision, and confidence.

This isn't just about better tools — it's about making your entire marketing strategy *smarter*. When you understand what your customers want and when they want it, everything else falls into place: your content, your offers, your sales.

Next Steps

If you haven't already, start by choosing one or two behavior-tracking tools — even a chatbot or simple heatmap — and begin collecting customer data. From there, layer in AI tools that cluster segments, analyze behavior, and trigger smart follow-ups.

In **Chapter 3: Smarter Content, Less Effort — AI-Powered Content Creation**, we'll show you how to turn those insights into high-performing content with half the effort. From blogs to emails to scripts, AI can help you create relevant, optimized material in minutes — without losing your voice.

Chapter 3: Smarter Content, Less Effort — AI-Powered Content Creation

Introduction

Creating content is the engine of modern marketing — blog posts, social captions, emails, landing pages, video scripts — all of it drives visibility, trust, and conversion. But for small and mid-sized businesses, keeping up with the content treadmill is exhausting. You either spend too much time writing, or too much money outsourcing, and still struggle to stay consistent.

Enter AI.

Artificial intelligence is transforming how content gets created. It's not just speeding things up — it's making content **more strategic, more personalized, and more scalable**. Today, even a one-person marketing team can produce high-performing content that sounds professional, ranks well in Google, and resonates with customers.

In this chapter, we'll break down exactly how SMBs can use AI to write faster, write smarter, and stay true to their brand voice — all while optimizing for both people and search engines.

How AI Can Help You Blog, Post, Email, and Script

Think of AI as your marketing assistant — one that never sleeps, constantly learns, and drafts content on command. Whether you're writing a weekly blog, a product launch email, or a YouTube script, AI tools can dramatically reduce the time and mental effort involved.

Where AI Adds Value in Content Creation

- **Idea Generation**: Give it a topic or product, and it can brainstorm angles, titles, or outlines
- **First Drafts**: Provide a few prompts and it writes initial versions of blog posts, emails, or ads
- **Repurposing Content**: Turn a blog post into social media snippets, a newsletter, or a video script
- **Content Scaling**: Need 10 product descriptions, fast? AI can produce them in seconds with consistency
- **A/B Testing Variants**: Easily generate multiple subject lines, headlines, or ad copies for testing

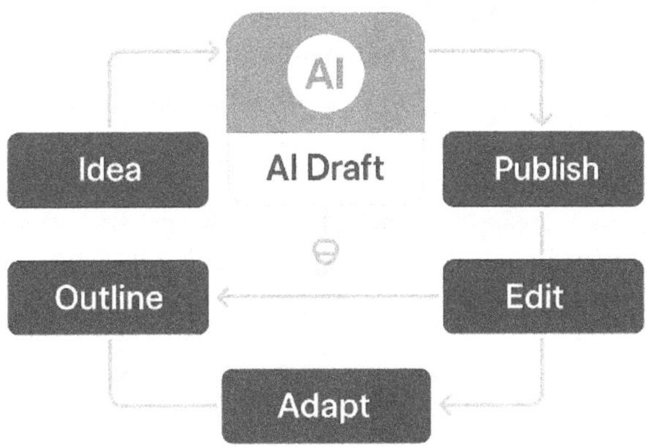

Real SMB Scenarios

- A real estate agent uses AI to generate weekly blog posts on local market trends
- A local bakery turns customer FAQs into automated email campaigns using AI
- A small coaching firm writes webinar scripts and landing pages in half the time

With AI, the bottleneck in content creation shifts from "how do we write this?" to "which version works best?"

Best Tools for AI-Powered Writing

There's no shortage of tools promising to write content for you, but not all are built for business use. Some are best for quick social posts. Others excel at long-form content or SEO. Choosing the right tools means knowing your needs — and your bandwidth.

Top AI Writing Tools for SMBs

- **ChatGPT**: Great for everything from blogs to chatbot replies; highly conversational and adaptable
- **Jasper**: Tailored for marketing content with templates for emails, blogs, landing pages, and ads
- **Copy.ai**: Fast, simple, and built for short-form copy like headlines, Instagram captions, or product blurbs
- **SurferSEO** (integrates with Jasper): Adds real-time SEO scoring and keyword guidance as you write

Features to Look For

- Templates for the type of content you need most
- Collaboration features for small teams
- Built-in editing and tone controls
- Export options or integrations with your CMS or email platform

Use Cases	Strengths	Pricing
ChatGPT	Conversational, versatile	Freemium
Jasper	Marketing, long-form content	$39/mo
Copy.ai	Brand voice, templates	Freemium
	Ease of use	Freemium

Tactical Tip

Don't choose a tool based on the longest list of features — choose the one that fits your **workflow** and gets you from draft to published faster.

Balancing AI with Your Voice

One of the biggest concerns we hear from business owners is this: *"Won't AI make my content sound robotic or generic?"*

The truth is — **only if you let it**.

AI is excellent at structure, speed, and grammar — but it's still your job to inject personality, values, and brand voice. Think of AI as a ghostwriter who needs direction. The more you guide it, the better the output.

How to Keep Your Voice in the Process

- **Provide Examples**: Show the tool past content or your tone preferences
- **Edit Strategically**: Let AI do the heavy lifting, then polish to match your voice
- **Use Custom Instructions**: Tools like ChatGPT allow you to specify tone ("friendly and expert" or "bold and concise")
- **Save and Reuse**: Build templates or tone profiles that reflect your brand — and reuse them

Common Use Cases Where Voice Still Matters

- CEO thought leadership posts
- Personalized customer emails
- Sales copy with emotional appeal
- Values-driven brand storytelling

Remember, AI is a tool. Your voice is the brand.

SEO Writing Hacks for Google and Readers

Search engine optimization (SEO) is one of the most valuable — and misunderstood — parts of content strategy. Too often, SMBs either ignore SEO completely or overdo it, stuffing keywords into lifeless copy. AI can help strike the balance.

With the right tools, AI can:

- **Suggest keywords** based on your topic and competition
- **Ensure readability** for humans and search engines alike
- **Maintain optimal structure** with headers, bullets, and meta descriptions
- **Check for duplicate content**, length issues, and overuse of phrases

Smart SEO Practices with AI

- Use AI to identify long-tail keywords — and then build content around those
- Let tools like SurferSEO or NeuronWriter give you content scores before publishing
- Include natural language questions in content (what, how, why) — these rank well in Google's featured snippets
- Balance internal linking with relevance — AI can suggest anchor text and placement

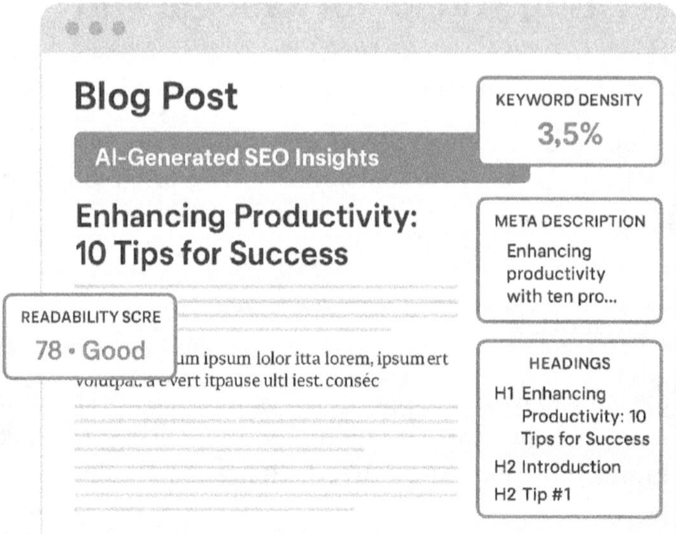

Avoid These SEO Mistakes

- Writing for bots instead of humans
- Ignoring search intent (what the reader *really* wants)
- Using too many keywords in unnatural ways
- Skipping content structure (no subheadings, long paragraphs)

Great SEO content isn't robotic. It's **relevant**, **well-structured**, and **valuable to the reader** — and AI helps you get there faster.

Real-World Example: Scaling Content with AI

Business Type: Small Accounting Firm
Challenge: Needed regular blogs and email newsletters but lacked internal writers
Old Approach:

- Inconsistent content output
- Outsourced articles that were often off-brand or late
- Low blog traffic and engagement

AI-Enhanced Approach:

- Used Jasper to create blog outlines and first drafts
- Editor polished drafts for tone and added localized tax info
- Used ChatGPT to repurpose blog posts into newsletter summaries and LinkedIn posts
- SurferSEO ensured all blogs were optimized for regional keywords

Results:

- Weekly blog cadence established
- Website traffic increased 58% in 3 months
- Email click-through rates doubled

Lesson: You don't need a big team — just a smart workflow.

Common Pitfalls to Avoid

- **Letting AI write without oversight**: Always review, edit, and apply your voice
- **Creating content for the sake of it**: Strategy still matters — focus on topics that move the needle
- **Ignoring reader experience**: Walls of AI-generated text won't convert — add formatting, images, and examples
- **Failing to train your tools**: Feed your AI inputs that reflect your tone and goals — it will improve over time

---

Conclusion

AI won't replace your marketing voice — but it will absolutely replace hours of repetitive writing, research, and editing. For SMBs, this is a massive win. Now you can stay consistent, scale output, and improve performance without burning out or blowing your budget.

Use AI for what it does best — structure, speed, and scale. Then bring in your human edge to make it memorable.

Next Steps

Start small: pick one recurring content task (like weekly social posts or a monthly email) and run it through an AI-powered workflow. Test, edit, and track results. Once you're confident, scale up to blogs, landing pages, and SEO.

In **Chapter 4: AI-Driven Social Media — From Chaos to Consistency**, we'll show you how to apply this same AI efficiency to your social channels — from scheduling posts at the perfect time to crafting viral-ready content and automating responses with smart bots.

Chapter 4: AI-Driven Social Media — From Chaos to Consistency

Introduction

Let's be honest: managing social media can feel like chasing a moving target — unpredictable algorithms, ever-shifting trends, and the constant pressure to be "always on." For SMBs, the result is often inconsistent posting, low engagement, and a scattered presence that fails to build real momentum.

AI is here to change that — not by adding more noise, but by adding **clarity, automation, and consistency**.

From predictive scheduling to intelligent caption generation and even AI-generated graphics, small businesses now have the power to turn their social media from a source of stress into a streamlined, strategic growth engine. You don't need a team of creatives or round-the-clock managers. You just need the right AI tools doing the heavy lifting.

This chapter walks you through exactly how SMBs are using AI to stay relevant, consistent, and customer-connected on social media — all while saving time and driving better results.

Scheduling + AI Timing Predictions

The best content in the world falls flat if it's posted at the wrong time. And guessing when your audience is active is just that — a guess. AI takes the guesswork out by analyzing patterns across your content history, follower behavior, and platform trends to recommend the **optimal times to post.**

How AI Scheduling Works

- **Behavioral Timing**: AI tools track when your audience is most active and likely to engage — by day, hour, and even device type.
- **Content Distribution**: AI spaces out content across platforms to avoid redundancy and optimize visibility.
- **Smart Reposting**: Tools like Buffer and Later use AI to re-share high-performing content at peak times for new segments.

Best Tools for AI Scheduling

- **Buffer** (AI time suggestions + performance scoring)
- **Later** (predictive engagement + calendar recommendations)
- **Lately.ai** (automatically pulls from long-form content to create dozens of optimized social posts)

Social Calendar

	Monday	Tuesday	Wednesday	Thursday	Friday	Sunday
9:00 AM	AI-imaget Engagement High	image Engagement Mialum	Image Engagement Medium	image Engagement Midium	image Engagement High	Content Mix Suggestion
12:00 PM	AI-imaget Engagement High	image Engagement Midium	Image Engagement Medium	image Engagement Midium	image Engagement High	Video Content Mix Suggestion
3:00 PM	AI-text Engagement Low	text Engagement Low	text Engagement Low	text Engagement Low	text Engagement Low	Suggest Content Mix Suggestion

Tactical Wins for SMBs

- Maintain a steady posting rhythm without daily manual work
- Post when your audience is *actually* online, not just when you remember
- Easily plan weeks of content in one sitting

How AI Analyzes Trends and Virality

Social media success today often hinges on **timing and trend awareness.** But it's impossible to monitor every platform, hashtag, and meme without help. That's where AI-driven social listening tools come in — tracking what's buzzing and identifying where your brand can plug in authentically.

What AI Social Trend Tools Do

- **Trend Detection**: Surface rising topics and hashtags in your niche before they peak
- **Sentiment Analysis**: Understand how people feel about a topic (positive, negative, neutral)
- **Competitive Tracking**: Monitor what competitors are posting and which content performs best
- **Virality Signals**: AI spots early engagement surges that predict what's about to take off

Popular AI Trend Monitoring Tools

- **BuzzSumo**: Identifies top-shared content and key influencers in your industry
- **Brand24**: Tracks mentions and sentiment across platforms
- **Exploding Topics**: Uses AI to surface up-and-coming search trends before they hit mainstream

Tactical Best Practices

- Create content around early signals — not tired trends
- Add value to trending conversations instead of just chasing them
- Set alerts for topics that align with your brand pillars

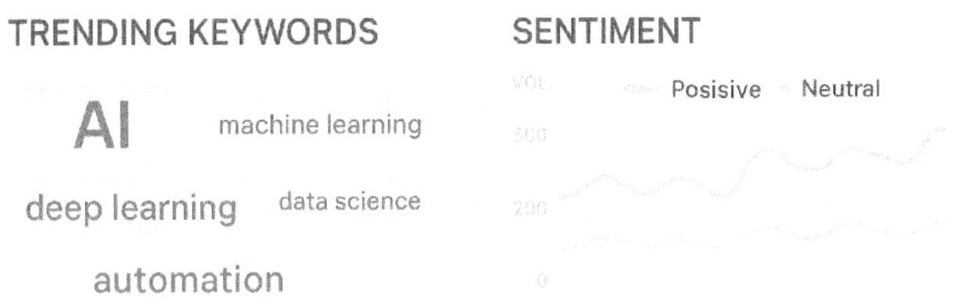

COMPETITOR POSTS COMPARISON

User	Posts	Likes	Comments
User	15	1,2K	300
Competitor A	12	800	150
Competitor B	18	1,5K	230
Competitor C	14	1K	180

Creating Engaging Captions and Images Using AI

You have seconds to grab attention on social media. Your caption needs to connect instantly. Your image needs to pop. And your message needs to convert — all in a 600x600 pixel square.

AI tools help you do this faster and better, with minimal creative fatigue.

AI for Captions

- **Copy.ai** and **Jasper**: Generate multiple caption options per post, tuned for humor, urgency, storytelling, or promotion
- **ChatGPT**: Drafts captions that match your tone, audience, and platform style — from Instagram to LinkedIn
- **Lately.ai**: Automatically generates social posts from longer content (blogs, podcasts, videos)

AI for Images

- **Canva Magic Design**: Suggests layouts, fonts, and visuals based on your content and style
- **Looka** and **Crello**: Auto-generate branded templates and visuals with minimal effort
- **DALL·E**: AI image generation that lets you create unique illustrations or thematic visuals from scratch

Real-World Use Case

A boutique skincare brand used AI to:

- Write 3 unique captions per Instagram post (storytelling, promo, education)
- Auto-generate visuals using Canva templates with branded colors and fonts
- Schedule content with predictive engagement timing via Later

Result: 78% increase in engagement in 60 days — with 1/3 the time investment.

Automating Social Customer Service with Bots

Customers don't just scroll on social — they ask questions, submit complaints, and seek help. Ignoring or delaying responses can cost you trust and sales.

AI-powered bots now make it possible to **respond instantly, route inquiries, and keep conversations flowing** without needing someone on call 24/7.

What Smart Bots Can Do

- **Auto-Respond**: Greet customers, answer FAQs, or collect contact info through Messenger, Instagram DMs, or web chat
- **Route to Humans**: Escalate complex issues to your team with full context
- **Personalize Responses**: Tailor answers based on user profile or previous interaction
- **Gather Feedback**: Use short surveys post-conversation to collect sentiment and improve support

Tools to Consider

- **ManyChat**: Build simple, automated flows for Instagram, Facebook, and WhatsApp
- **MobileMonkey**: Connects chat flows across platforms with AI logic
- **Tidio**: Combines chatbot + live chat with smart triggers and workflows

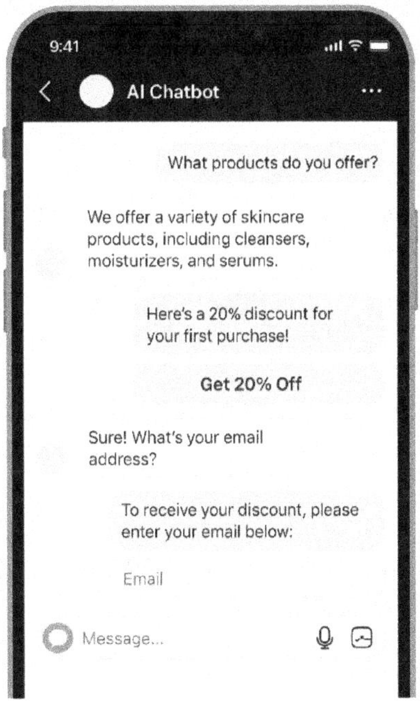

Tactical Wins for SMBs

- Reduce response time from hours to seconds
- Keep leads engaged even after hours
- Turn support interactions into conversion opportunities

Real-World Example: AI-Supported Social Strategy

Business Type: Local Outdoor Gear Shop
Challenge: Inconsistent posting, low engagement, slow response times on DMs
Old Approach:

- Manual posts 1–2x/week based on intuition
- Replies handled once a day (or missed entirely)
- Low visibility, no growth in followers

AI-Driven Approach:

- Used Lately.ai to extract dozens of social posts from blog content
- Scheduled all posts using Buffer's AI-timed calendar
- Installed ManyChat to automate DMs and collect emails from prospects
- Used BuzzSumo to stay on top of hiking gear trends

Results:

- 3x increase in post frequency with no extra team
- Response time under 5 minutes, 24/7
- 46% increase in social-driven revenue in 3 months

Common Pitfalls to Avoid

- **Posting without planning**: AI helps, but strategy still matters — build a monthly content calendar
- **Over-automating**: Humanize where it matters (especially in responses)
- **Chasing every trend**: Not every viral topic fits your brand — pick your moments
- **Ignoring analytics**: Track what works and evolve — AI improves with feedback loops

---

Conclusion

AI isn't just a time-saver for social media — it's a game-changer for visibility, engagement, and customer connection. For SMBs, this means more than just getting posts out on time. It means showing up consistently, saying the right things, and staying tuned into what your audience cares about.

When AI powers the backend — from scheduling to replies — you get to focus on what really matters: building a brand people trust and follow.

Next Steps

Start by reviewing your current social media process. What's taking too long? What's falling through the cracks? Then select one AI tool for scheduling and one for content — and begin testing.

In **Chapter 5: Email Marketing that Converts — Built with AI**, we'll take the same level of automation and personalization into your inbox strategy. Learn how AI boosts open rates, re-engages cold leads, and delivers smarter campaigns through segmentation, testing, and timing — all tailored to each recipient.

Chapter 5: Email Marketing that Converts — Built with AI

Introduction

Email marketing has long been one of the most reliable drivers of ROI — but that doesn't mean it's easy to get right. Too many small and mid-sized businesses fall into the trap of sending one-size-fits-all messages that go unopened, unnoticed, or directly into the spam folder.

The reason? **Lack of relevance, timing, and personalization.**

This is exactly where AI steps in. Today's AI-powered email tools enable businesses to segment smarter, personalize deeper, and automate campaigns that feel tailored to each individual recipient — even if you're managing a list of thousands.

In this chapter, we'll break down how AI transforms email from a generic blast into a precision communication tool. You'll see how to boost open rates, click-throughs, and conversions by using intelligent segmentation, predictive analytics, and real-time optimization — without adding to your workload.

Smart Segmentation & Personalization

The days of sending the same email to your entire list are over. With AI, segmentation goes beyond age or location — it considers **behavior, purchase patterns, engagement history, and even content preferences**.

How AI Builds Smarter Segments

- **Behavioral Segmentation**: AI tools automatically group users by browsing history, email opens, or product interactions.
- **Predictive Scoring**: Assigns a likelihood to take action — purchase, unsubscribe, re-engage — based on past behavior.
- **Real-Time Personalization**: Emails can dynamically adjust content blocks (product offers, images, messaging) to match recipient profiles.

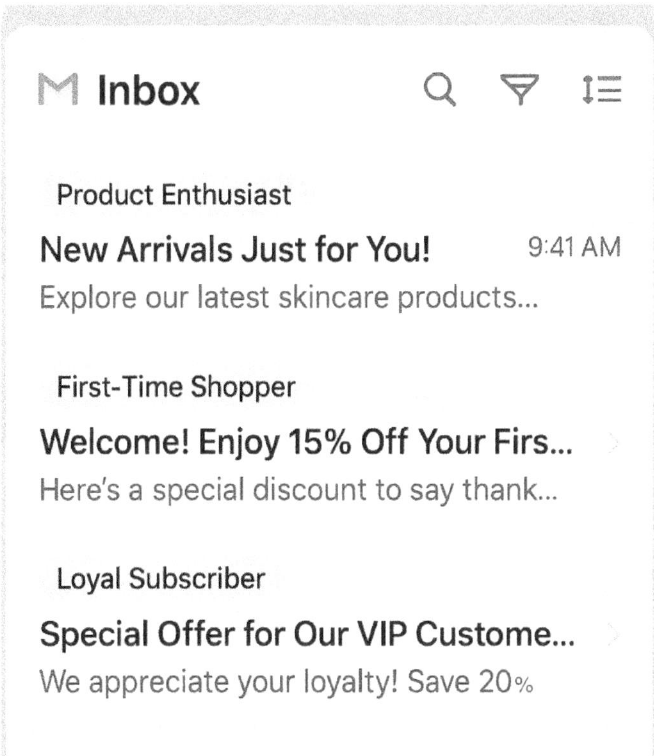

Practical Example

A small online bookstore uses AI to:

- Segment readers into genres based on past purchases (mystery, romance, nonfiction)
- Send weekly recommendations featuring books in the recipient's preferred genre
- Automatically insert first names, local events, and custom discount codes

Result: Open rates jumped from 18% to 41% and repeat purchases doubled.

A/B Testing Subject Lines, Send Times, and CTA Buttons

Traditional A/B testing is valuable, but slow — and often inconclusive due to small sample sizes or manual setups. AI supercharges this process by testing multiple variables at once and learning from engagement patterns across your entire audience.

AI Testing Features

- **Multi-Variant Subject Line Testing**: Generate and test multiple subject lines in real time; AI adjusts future sends based on performance
- **Send Time Optimization**: AI predicts the exact time a recipient is most likely to open, and schedules accordingly
- **Smart CTAs**: AI tools can vary button color, wording, and placement — and serve the best version automatically

Best Practices

- Let AI tools test *and learn continuously* — don't just run one-off tests
- Use subject line testing in every campaign — it's the lowest-effort, highest-impact optimization
- Pair CTA testing with heatmap data to understand what drives action

A/B Test Performance ● Live

Subject Line	Open Rate	CTA	Click Rate
Don't Miss Our Sale! Explore our latest Sale	45.2%	Shop Now	8.1%
Shop Our Exclusive Sale Open rate	48.5%	Browse Sale	9.4%
Variation C Clck Rate	7.5%	9:00 AM 3:00 PM	7.9%

Predicting Churn and Re-Engagement Flows

Every list has inactive subscribers. The key is knowing *when* they're slipping — and what to do about it.

AI models can track early signals of disengagement and automatically trigger **re-engagement workflows**, sending the right message before a lead goes cold or unsubscribes.

What to Watch

- **Drop in open/click rate over 3+ sends**
- **No site visits in 30–60 days**
- **Lower interaction than segment peers**

Re-Engagement Triggers You Can Automate

- **"We miss you" campaigns** with personalized offers
- **Feedback surveys** asking why they've disengaged
- **Product recommendations** based on past interests
- **Last-chance alerts** before suppressing the contact

Real-World Example

An email list cleaning company used Sender's AI engine to flag subscribers showing low engagement for 90+ days. It launched a 3-step re-engagement sequence with product tips and a 10% discount.

Outcome: 27% of flagged users reactivated, reducing list churn and boosting ROI per campaign.

Tools: Mailchimp AI, Sender, Moosend

These tools don't just help you send emails — they help you **send smarter emails**. Here's how the top platforms compare for SMB use:

Mailchimp AI

- **Best For**: All-in-one marketing automation
- **AI Features**: Send time optimization, content suggestions, predictive analytics
- **Extras**: Product recommendations for eCommerce

Sender

- **Best For**: Affordable automation with AI insights
- **AI Features**: Email scoring, smart re-engagement flows, personalization tags
- **Extras**: Built-in heatmaps and visual builder

Moosend

- **Best For**: Segmentation-heavy campaigns
- **AI Features**: Behavioral triggers, product-based dynamic content, A/B testing automation
- **Extras**: Drag-and-drop automation builder, WooCommerce/Shopify integrations

Feature	Mailchimp AI	Sender	Moosend
Personalization	✓	✓	✓
Automation	✓		✓
Testing	✓	✓	
			✓

Choosing the Right Tool

Pick a platform that:

- Integrates with your eCommerce or CRM system
- Supports your list size and growth goals
- Offers AI-powered insights (not just automation)

Real-World Case Study: Rebuilding Email ROI with AI

Business Type: Regional Wellness Center
Challenge: Declining open rates and low booking conversions
Old Approach: Weekly promotional emails sent to the entire list at 10 a.m. Tuesdays

AI-Enhanced Approach:

- Switched to Moosend for smart segmentation
- Let AI test 5 subject lines per campaign
- Used past booking data to segment offers by class type (yoga, strength, meditation)
- Automated send times based on historical engagement per user
- Built a reactivation sequence for disengaged subscribers

Results:

- 3x increase in click-through rate
- 41% increase in bookings from email
- Churn reduced by 22% in three months

Common Pitfalls to Avoid

- **Using only first-name personalization**: True personalization is about behavior, not just tokens
- **Sending too often (or too little)**: AI can help find the balance — trust the data
- **Ignoring performance feedback**: AI learns best with input — track opens, clicks, bounces
- **Forgetting mobile**: Over 60% of email is read on phones — optimize design accordingly

Conclusion

AI-powered email marketing isn't just a "nice-to-have" — it's quickly becoming essential for any SMB serious about conversion. With AI handling the heavy lifting — from segmentation to timing to testing — your emails become more relevant, more timely, and more effective.

Done right, your list becomes more than a database — it becomes a conversion engine.

Next Steps

Start with a quick audit of your current email tool. Are you still sending the same email to everyone? If so, prioritize a platform with built-in AI segmentation and timing. Then launch a small A/B test campaign and track what happens.

In **Chapter 6: AI in Ad Campaigns — Get More Clicks for Less**, we'll explore how AI takes paid advertising to the next level — helping you launch dynamic, optimized ads across Facebook, Google, and LinkedIn while spending less per click and finding customers who actually convert.

Chapter 6: AI in Ad Campaigns — Get More Clicks for Less

Introduction

Advertising has always been a powerful lever for growth — but for many small and mid-sized businesses, it can feel like a black hole of budget. You boost a post, run a Google ad, and hope for the best. Meanwhile, costs creep up, results stay murky, and your time disappears into dashboards and guesswork.

AI flips this on its head.

Today's ad platforms are built on AI. The winners are no longer the businesses with the biggest budgets — they're the ones using **smart automation, intelligent targeting, and real-time optimization**. That means ads that perform better, cost less, and get in front of the right people at the right time.

In this chapter, we'll unpack how to use AI to design, launch, and optimize ad campaigns across Facebook, Google, and LinkedIn — without being an ad expert. Whether you're running your first campaign or scaling your fifth, you'll learn how to drive more clicks for less money using the same tools top marketers trust.

AI Ad Optimization for Facebook, Google, and LinkedIn

Most major ad platforms are already built on AI — but unless you know how to work with those systems, you're leaving money on the table. AI ad optimization means trusting the algorithm to do what it's built for: **test, learn, and improve** — faster than any human could.

What AI Ad Platforms Automatically Handle

- **Audience learning**: AI identifies who's most likely to click or convert — then narrows in over time
- **Bid adjustments**: Raises or lowers your ad bids based on real-time competition and performance
- **Creative delivery**: Shows the right combination of headline, image, and call-to-action to each viewer

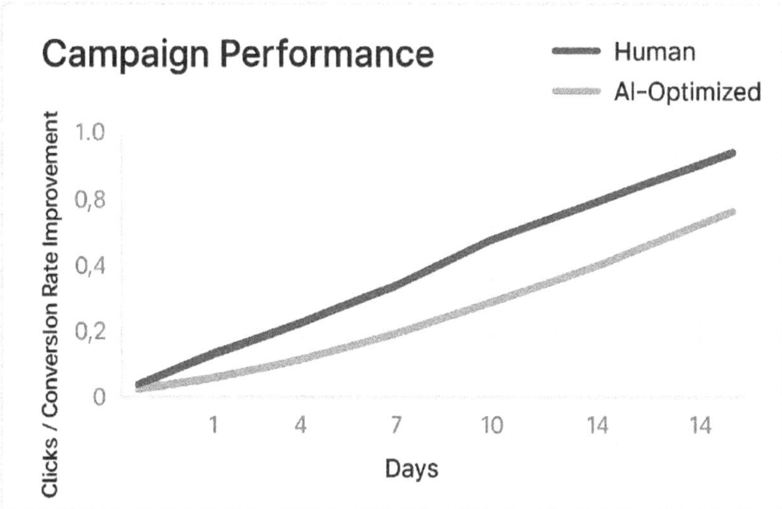

How to Leverage AI on Each Platform

- **Facebook/Instagram (Meta Ads)**: Use Advantage+ placements and allow broad targeting — let the AI find best-fit users
- **Google Ads**: Use Performance Max campaigns for automatic channel selection, asset testing, and conversion tracking
- **LinkedIn Ads**: AI-driven bidding and dynamic ad copy for job title, industry, and company size

Pro Tip: Avoid micromanaging. The more flexibility you give the algorithm (in budget and audience), the faster it learns.

Dynamic Ads Tailored in Real-Time

Dynamic ads adapt based on who's viewing them — showing different products, copy, or images based on location, behavior, or stage in the customer journey. AI makes this possible at scale, without manually creating dozens of variations.

How Dynamic Ads Work

- **Ecommerce Example**: Someone who viewed a blue hiking backpack gets an ad showing that exact product, with a time-sensitive discount
- **Service Business Example**: A returning visitor sees a "limited availability" message, while a new lead sees a free consultation offer
- **B2B Example**: Different LinkedIn users see industry-specific stats in the ad copy, based on their profile data

Tools That Support Dynamic Ads

- **Meta Advantage+ Catalog Ads**
- **Google Smart Shopping and Performance Max**
- **LinkedIn Dynamic Ads (job-based personalization)**

Result: Higher relevance, better click-through rates, and stronger ROI — without extra production work.

Geo-Targeting and Lookalike Audiences

Reaching the right people is just as important as saying the right thing. AI gives you two powerful options: **geo-targeting** and **lookalike modeling**.

Geo-Targeting with AI

AI identifies where your audience is most likely to convert — not just by city or zip code, but by behavior clusters. This means you can:

- Focus spend on regions with high conversion probability
- Exclude low-performing geos in real time
- Adjust offers or headlines by region ("NYC Clients Get 15% Off Today")

Lookalike Audiences

A lookalike audience is a group of new users who "look" like your best customers — based on dozens (or hundreds) of shared traits.

AI builds these audiences by analyzing:

- Purchase history
- Website behavior
- Demographics
- Engagement with past ads

Where to Use Them

- **Facebook**: Create lookalikes based on email list, web traffic, or past converters
- **Google Ads**: Similar audiences for search, display, and video campaigns
- **LinkedIn**: Account-based lookalikes for targeting decision-makers in similar industries

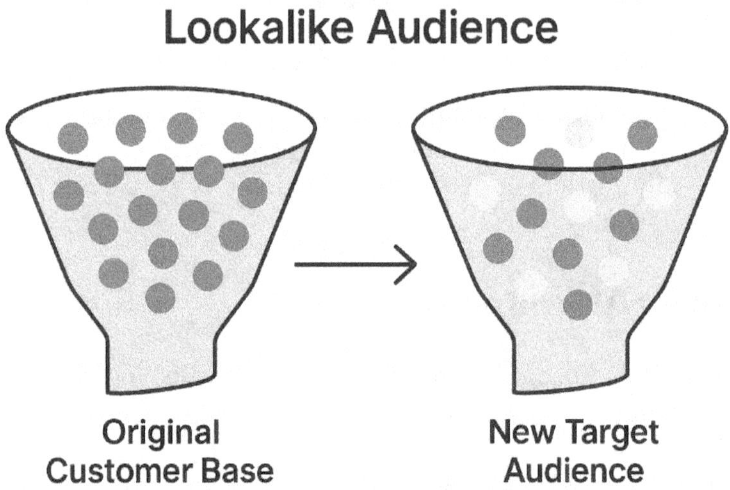

Tactical Tip: Refresh lookalikes every 30–60 days to stay relevant and avoid audience fatigue.

Ad Copy & Design Suggestions from AI Tools

You no longer need a copywriter or designer to test five versions of an ad. AI tools can generate copy variations, suggest imagery, and even adjust tone — helping you iterate faster and with confidence.

Best Tools for SMBs

- **Copy.ai**: Quickly generate headlines, body text, and CTAs for any type of ad
- **Jasper**: Ideal for multi-platform campaigns — integrates tone, product details, and hooks
- **Canva Magic Design**: Suggests layouts and visuals based on your brand and content
- **AdCreative.ai**: Generates entire ad sets (images, copy, format) using AI insights

How to Use AI Copy Effectively

- Input your target audience and campaign goal
- Generate 5–10 variations
- Test 2–3 at a time in platform (Meta, Google, etc.)
- Let AI optimize delivery based on performance

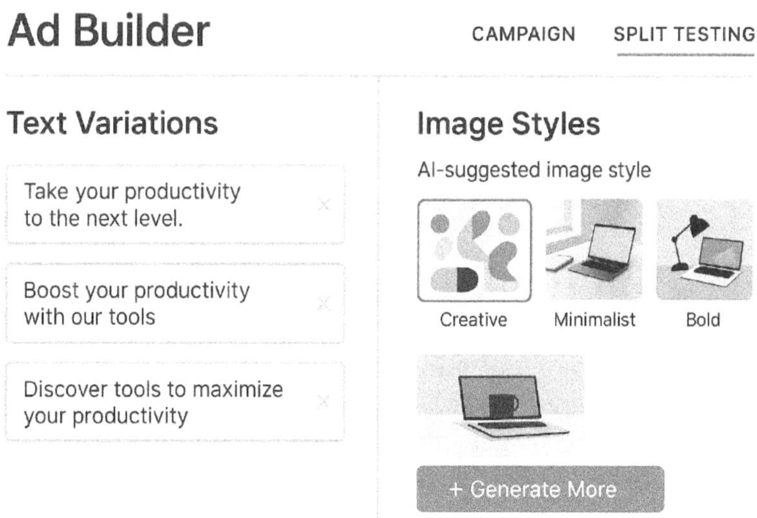

Pro Tip: Don't settle on the first version. Use AI to generate quantity, then apply human judgment to refine quality.

Real-World Example: Getting More for Less with AI Ads

Business Type: Local Event Venue
Challenge: High cost per click on Facebook ads, low return on ad spend (ROAS)
Old Approach:

- Targeted local radius with one static image and ad
- Manual bid settings, generic headline
- Cost per click: $2.94 | ROAS: 1.2x

AI-Enhanced Approach:

- Switched to Meta Advantage+ campaigns
- Used lookalike audiences based on past bookers
- Generated 10 ad copy variants using Copy.ai
- Let AI select placements and automatically optimize bids

New Results:

- Cost per click: $0.89
- ROAS: 4.7x
- 3x more bookings in 30 days with the same budget

Common Pitfalls to Avoid

- **Over-narrow targeting**: Give the algorithm enough data to learn and optimize
- **Setting and forgetting**: AI needs monitoring — check performance weekly and adjust creatives
- **Ignoring copy**: Great visuals help, but strong messaging drives action
- **Skipping mobile preview**: Most clicks happen on mobile — test and design accordingly

Conclusion

AI has turned ad campaigns from guesswork into guided systems. It doesn't just automate — it **learns**. For SMBs, this means you no longer need deep ad expertise to get results. With the right tools and mindset, you can create campaigns that perform better, scale faster, and cost less.

Let the AI handle the complexity. You focus on strategy, voice, and business outcomes.

Next Steps

Pick one channel — Facebook, Google, or LinkedIn — and run a small AI-powered campaign using broad targeting, dynamic creative, and automated placements. Use tools like Copy.ai or AdCreative.ai to support the creative process, and track results against previous efforts.

In **Chapter 7: Building Funnels with AI — From Click to Customer**, we'll show you how to turn those ad clicks into paying customers. You'll learn how to map the full customer journey, optimize landing pages, and automate follow-ups — even if you're not technical.

Chapter 7: Building Funnels with AI — From Click to Customer

Introduction

You've run the ad, posted the content, and maybe even captured a click — but what happens next? For many SMBs, this is where the trail goes cold. Visitors bounce. Leads go quiet. Potential customers slip through the cracks, not because of poor marketing, but because the path forward isn't clear or optimized.

This is the job of your funnel — the system that guides someone from *curious clicker* to *committed buyer*. And with AI, you can now design, test, and optimize these journeys without needing a technical background or full-time marketing staff.

AI-powered funnel building means smarter lead capture, better landing pages, automatic nurturing, and real-time insights — all tailored to customer behavior. In this chapter, we'll show how AI makes the complex simple, helping SMBs build funnels that actually *convert*.

Mapping Your Customer Journey with AI Tools

Before you build a funnel, you need to understand the journey. Who is your visitor? Where do they come from? What do they care about? What objections might stop them from buying?

AI tools help you answer these questions by analyzing customer behavior across channels — showing you **where friction exists and where to improve flow**.

AI Tools for Journey Mapping

- **Funnelytics**: Visual journey mapping with real-time conversion data
- **HubSpot CRM with AI Insights**: Tracks engagement across emails, ads, forms, and pages
- **Google Analytics + Predictive AI**: Identifies high-exit pages, conversion paths, and drop-off patterns

What You Can Learn

- Where users land and where they drop off
- Which content or step triggers action
- How long the journey takes — and where it stalls

Pro Tip: Don't guess the journey — **observe** it. Let data shape your funnel, not assumptions.

Landing Page Optimization with AI (Unbounce, Instapage)

Landing pages are the workhorses of any funnel. But for non-designers and busy SMBs, building high-converting pages can be a struggle. AI now makes it possible to generate, test, and optimize landing pages without coding — and with impressive results.

Top AI-Driven Platforms

- **Unbounce Smart Builder**:
  - Suggests layouts based on your goal (leads, sales, event signups)
  - Dynamically adjusts headlines based on visitor intent
  - A/B tests multiple versions automatically
- **Instapage AI Personalization**:
  - Serves different copy/images based on location, ad clicked, or industry
  - Tracks engagement and adjusts design elements in real time

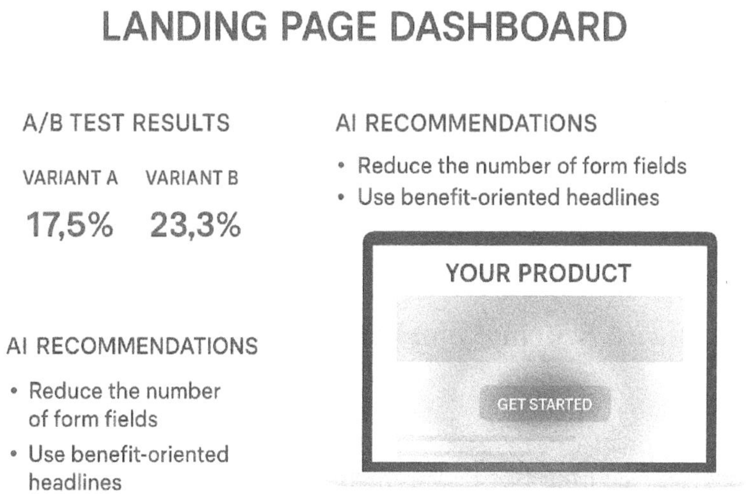

Key Benefits for SMBs

- No need to hire a designer or developer
- Speed to launch: pages built in under an hour
- Smart suggestions that improve over time
- Personalization that feels relevant to each visitor

Example: A fitness coach using Unbounce saw a 42% lift in sign-ups by switching from a static landing page to an AI-optimized one that changed testimonials based on the user's city.

Automated Lead Scoring and Nurturing

Once you've captured a lead, you need to know two things:
1. Are they ready to buy?
2. If not, how do you guide them until they are?

AI helps you prioritize leads through predictive scoring and nurture them through tailored, automated sequences — based on real behavior, not just timelines.

How AI Lead Scoring Works

- Assigns points to actions: email opens, page visits, webinar sign-ups, etc.
- Uses machine learning to detect high-converting behaviors
- Flags when a lead becomes "sales-ready" — or at risk of dropping off

Nurturing with AI

- Tools like **ActiveCampaign** or **HubSpot** trigger sequences based on behavior (not just days since signup)
- Emails and offers adjust automatically to match user interest level
- Dynamic content keeps leads engaged without manual effort

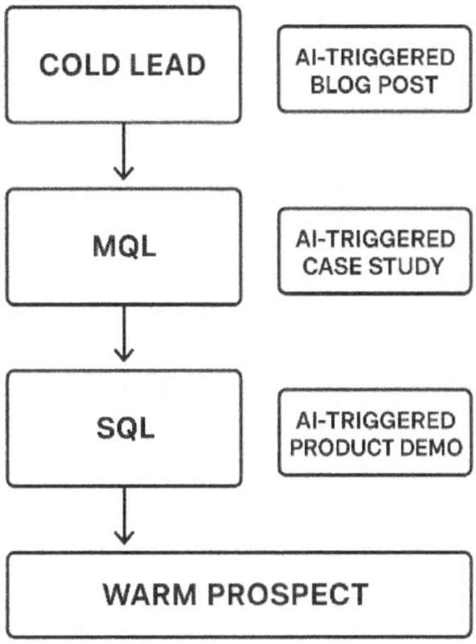

This image is a **lead funnel flowchart** that visually outlines how a lead progresses through stages from a **cold lead** to a **warm prospect**, with **AI-triggered content** at each step:

1. **Cold Lead**
   → Receives an **AI-triggered blog post** to spark initial interest.
2. **MQL (Marketing Qualified Lead)**
   → Gets an **AI-triggered case study** to deepen engagement.

3. **SQL (Sales Qualified Lead)**
   → Shown an **AI-triggered product demo** to encourage conversion.
4. **Warm Prospect**
   → Final stage indicating the lead is ready for sales action.

Arrows indicate the linear progression, and each AI-triggered action is shown alongside the corresponding lead stage. The style is minimalist, using bold text inside clean rectangles with light directional flow.

Real SMB Example

A professional services firm used AI-based scoring in Moosend. Once a lead hit 80 points (opened 3+ emails, viewed pricing page), they received a personalized proposal. Those under 40 points entered a nurture track with case studies and educational content.

Outcome: 3x increase in proposal acceptance rate and fewer lost leads.

Funnel-Building Without Being a Techie

You don't need to write code, configure servers, or hire a team of developers. Today's AI tools are designed for business owners, marketers, and solopreneurs — with **drag-and-drop simplicity and smart automation built-in.**

Build a Complete Funnel Using:

1. **Landing Page**: Built with Unbounce or Instapage
2. **Form + CRM**: Capture info and send to HubSpot, Mailchimp, or ActiveCampaign
3. **Lead Scoring + Automation**: Triggered via CRM or integrated AI tools
4. **Follow-up Emails**: Written by Jasper or Copy.ai, personalized via AI
5. **Analytics Dashboard**: Monitored via Funnelytics or Google Analytics AI layer

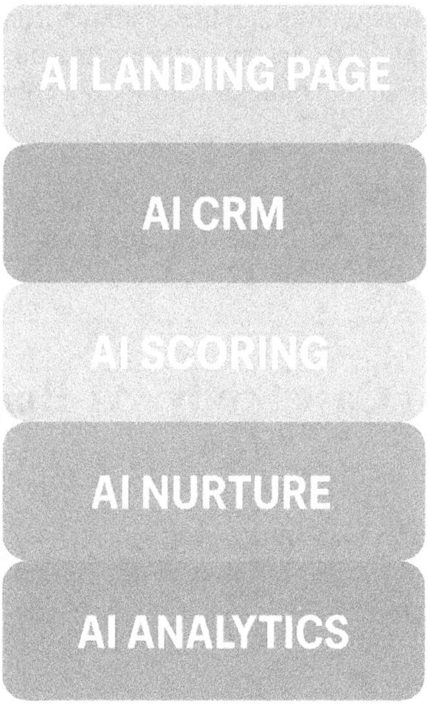

This image presents a **visual stack of AI-powered tools** used in a typical marketing and sales workflow. Each layer of the stack represents a specific function:

1. **AI Landing Page** – the top layer, responsible for attracting and converting visitors.
2. **AI CRM** – centralizes customer data and interactions.
3. **AI Scoring** – ranks leads based on behavioral and engagement data.
4. **AI Nurture** – automates personalized follow-up and content delivery.
5. **AI Analytics** – monitors performance and provides insights at the bottom layer.

The stack's colors transition smoothly from light blue to teal, symbolizing progression through the customer lifecycle—from acquisition to insight. The design is clean, structured, and ideal for illustrating how these tools integrate to form a cohesive AI marketing engine.

You can build your first complete funnel in a day — and improve it over time as AI learns and refines your process.

Real-World Case Study: AI-Built Funnel Success

Business Type: B2B Consulting Firm
Challenge: Poor conversion from paid ads and no clear lead qualification system
Old Approach:

- Ads pointed to homepage
- Manual email follow-up with all leads
- No tracking of lead quality or funnel drop-off

AI-Enhanced Funnel:

- Used Instapage to create audience-specific landing pages (by industry)
- Installed HubSpot CRM with AI-based lead scoring
- Connected Jasper-generated email sequences for nurturing
- Monitored drop-offs using Funnelytics

Results:

- Conversion rate increased from 1.9% to 5.6%
- 50% reduction in unqualified leads passed to sales
- Sales team reported 3x improvement in lead "readiness"

Common Pitfalls to Avoid

- **Overcomplicating your funnel**: Start simple — one path, one CTA, one goal
- **Ignoring lead signals**: Track engagement, not just submissions
- **Failing to connect tools**: Your funnel is only as strong as its integrations
- **Building for yourself, not your audience**: Let behavior and data guide your design

Conclusion

Building high-converting funnels used to require big teams, big budgets, or both. Now, thanks to AI, any business can design smart, scalable customer journeys — tailored to behavior, optimized for conversion, and automated from end to end.

With the right tools, you don't need to be a tech expert. You just need to think like a guide: lead your customers down the path they're already trying to take.

Next Steps

Pick one campaign — an offer, service, or product — and map out the steps from first click to final conversion. Use AI tools like Unbounce and ActiveCampaign to build a simple funnel, then refine it using journey analytics.

In **Chapter 8: Analytics Without the Headache — AI Makes It Easy**, we'll explore how AI helps you track what matters, predict what's next, and turn your marketing data into decisions that actually drive growth.

Chapter 8: Analytics Without the Headache — AI Makes It Easy

Introduction

If you've ever stared at a marketing dashboard and wondered, "What am I supposed to *do* with this?", you're not alone. For most SMBs, analytics feels like a tangle of charts, vanity metrics, and technical jargon. You know you need data to improve performance — but which data actually matters?

That's where AI makes all the difference.

AI-powered analytics strip away the noise and surface **actionable insights**, not just raw numbers. It doesn't just tell you *what happened*, but also *what's likely to happen next* — and even recommends next steps.

In this chapter, we'll show how small and mid-sized businesses can use AI-enhanced tools to simplify tracking, improve ROI, and make confident, data-backed decisions — without getting buried in spreadsheets.

AI Dashboards That Show *What Matters*

Traditional analytics tools like Google Analytics or basic email metrics often leave business owners guessing. You see bounce rates, page views, and clicks — but not *why* things are happening or what to change.

AI dashboards change the game. They summarize massive data sets into **clear visual insights** and automatically highlight the trends that matter most.

What AI Dashboards Do Differently

- **Surface Key Trends**: Flag underperforming campaigns, rising customer segments, or product interest spikes
- **Contextual Alerts**: "Your landing page conversion rate dropped 22% this week — visitors are spending 40% less time on it."
- **Custom KPIs**: Adjust based on your business model — whether you care most about email signups, bookings, or average order value

Tools That Deliver This Clarity

- **Google Analytics 4 + AI insights**: Offers predictive audience behavior and deeper attribution tracking
- **Piwik PRO**: Privacy-friendly, customizable dashboards with real-time AI analysis
- **Zoho Analytics or Looker Studio (with AI layers)**: Combine multiple data sources into a single intelligent dashboard

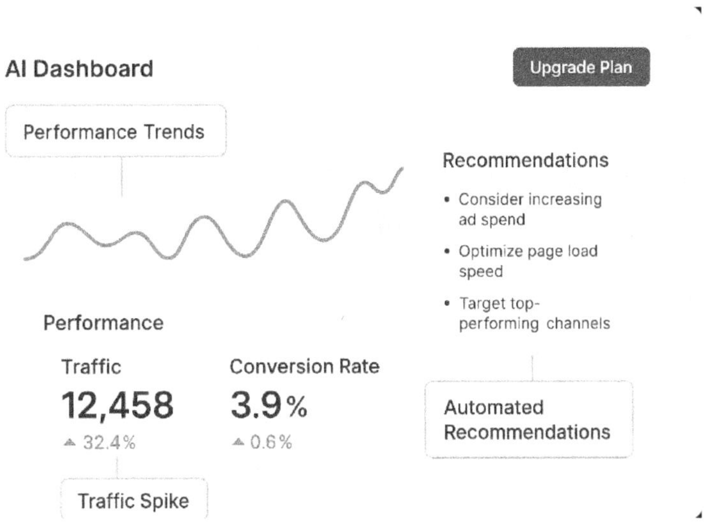

This AI dashboard image displays a well-annotated interface summarizing key performance metrics for digital marketing or web analytics.

Summary:

- **Performance Trends:** A line chart shows user activity patterns over time.
- **Traffic Spike:** A highlighted section notes a rise to 12,458 visitors (+32.4%).
- **Conversion Rate:** Listed at 3.9%, with a 0.6% increase.
- **Automated Recommendations:** AI-generated suggestions include increasing ad spend, optimizing page speed, and targeting top-performing channels.

The layout is clean and professional, with highlighted callouts making it ideal for showcasing insights during a performance review.

Pro Tip: Choose a tool that fits your business type — not just your ad channels.

Predictive Metrics: What Will Happen Next?

Reporting what *already happened* is helpful — but being able to forecast what's likely to happen is where AI shines. Predictive analytics use past behavior, historical trends, and real-time engagement to show where your marketing is headed.

What AI Can Predict

- **Which leads are likely to convert**
- **Which products or content will trend next**
- **When customer churn is most likely**
- **How much revenue a campaign will generate based on current pace**

How This Works for SMBs

- A local restaurant chain uses AI to forecast busy days based on weather, foot traffic, and reservation patterns
- A coaching firm sees which email subscribers are most likely to book a session based on click patterns and page time
- An eCommerce store identifies which inactive customers are most likely to re-engage with a discount

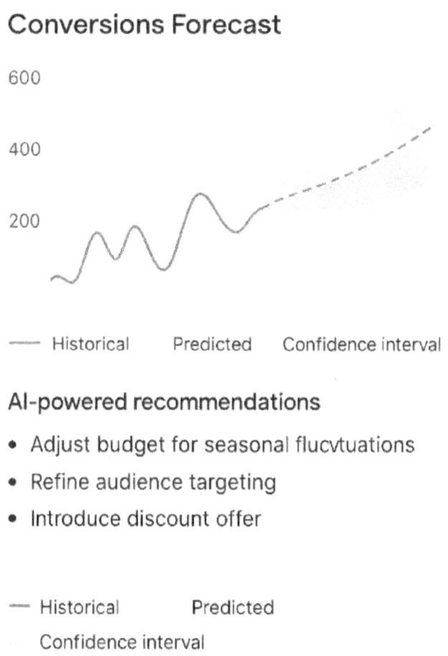

This image is a **conversions forecast dashboard** powered by AI. It visualizes historical and predicted conversion rates over time:

- **Historical Data**: Solid blue line showing past conversions.
- **Predicted Data**: Dashed blue line projecting future conversions.
- **Confidence Interval**: A shaded blue range that indicates possible fluctuation in forecasted values.

Below the graph, AI-powered recommendations suggest:

- Adjusting budget for seasonal fluctuations
- Refining audience targeting
- Introducing a discount offer

This dashboard helps marketers plan proactively with both insight and confidence.

Tactical Tip: Start with one prediction — like customer churn or email opens — and use it to guide a small campaign experiment.

Real Examples of SMBs Improving ROI Using AI Insights

Case Study 1: Subscription Box Business

Challenge: Plateaued growth and stagnant customer LTV
Solution: Used AI analytics to segment customers by reorder behavior
Action: Created early-upgrade offers for high-LTV segments
Result: Increased revenue per user by 23% in 60 days

Case Study 2: Regional Marketing Agency

Challenge: Clients overwhelmed by traditional campaign reports
Solution: Switched to Looker Studio dashboards with AI-generated summaries
Action: Clients received weekly "What's Working" snapshots with clear next steps
Result: Higher client retention and faster campaign turnaround

Case Study 3: Boutique Fashion Store

Challenge: High cart abandonment, no clarity on causes
Solution: Piwik PRO AI flagged slow-loading product pages as a drop-off driver
Action: Optimized image sizes, personalized cart emails based on abandoned items
Result: Reduced abandonment by 38%, boosted conversions by 19%

BEFORE AI	AFTER AI
12,500 Clicks	**18,200** ↑ 46%
3.2% Conversion Rate	**5.0%** ↑ 56%
$25,000 Revenue	**$42,000** ↑ 68%

This side-by-side comparison image titled **"Before AI vs. After AI"** showcases measurable improvements in three key performance metrics after AI implementation:

- **Clicks** increased from 12,500 to 18,200 — a **46% improvement**.
- **Conversion Rate** rose from 3.2% to 5.0% — a **56% increase**.
- **Revenue** grew from $25,000 to $42,000 — a **68% gain**.

Each value is clearly labeled, with green arrows and percentages indicating positive changes. This visual snapshot effectively highlights the ROI and impact of using AI in marketing or business performance.

Tools: Piwik PRO, Google Analytics + AI Layers

Here's a quick breakdown of top AI-friendly tools for SMB analytics:

Piwik PRO

- **Best For**: Privacy-conscious businesses (GDPR/CCPA compliant)
- **AI Features**: On-site behavior insights, real-time funnels, conversion probability
- **Why It Works**: Ideal for healthcare, education, or regulated industries

Google Analytics 4

- **Best For**: Businesses already using Google Ads, Search Console, and YouTube
- **AI Features**: Predictive audiences (likely to convert), churn forecasts, automated insights
- **Why It Works**: Unified tracking across web and apps, strong integrations

Looker Studio (formerly Data Studio) + AI Layers

- **Best For**: Custom dashboards for multiple data sources (email, ads, sales)
- **AI Features**: Visualization of AI-generated insights from integrated platforms
- **Why It Works**: Flexible, customizable, visual — ideal for agencies and cross-channel marketers

Use Case	Piwik PRO	GA4	Looker Studio
Privacy	✓	–	–
Prediction	–	✓	✓
Customization	✓	✓	✓
Integration	✓	✓	✓

Common Pitfalls to Avoid

- **Tracking everything, understanding nothing**: Focus on 3–5 metrics that tie directly to your goals
- **Skipping setup**: GA4 and similar tools need proper configuration to track conversions, events, and goals accurately
- **Ignoring mobile insights**: Over half of traffic comes from mobile — segment performance by device
- **Treating AI suggestions as gospel**: AI insights are powerful, but still need human interpretation

Conclusion

AI makes analytics usable — not just available. Instead of drowning in dashboards or second-guessing reports, you now have the tools to understand performance at a glance, spot patterns before they become problems, and make decisions that actually move your business forward.

No more spreadsheets. No more stress. Just smart data that helps you grow.

Next Steps

Start by reviewing your current analytics setup. Are you looking at raw data, or actionable insights? Choose one AI-enhanced tool — even if it's just GA4 — and enable automated alerts or predictive features. Use those signals to improve one campaign or page this week.

In **Chapter 9: Ethics, Bias & Trust — Marketing AI the Right Way**, we'll shift from what AI *can* do to what it *should* do. You'll learn how to build trust, avoid biased targeting, and use automation responsibly — because great marketing is not just effective, it's ethical.

Chapter 9: Ethics, Bias & Trust — Marketing AI the Right Way

Introduction

As AI becomes more integrated into how small businesses attract, engage, and convert customers, there's one essential truth we can't afford to ignore:

Just because you *can* do something with AI doesn't always mean you *should.*

In today's fast-moving digital landscape, trust is everything. Consumers are more aware — and more wary — of how their data is used, how they're being targeted, and whether the experiences they receive are helpful… or just plain creepy.

That's why ethical AI marketing isn't a luxury or PR strategy — it's a **core business requirement**. Especially for SMBs, where customer relationships are more personal, any misuse of automation can damage trust, brand reputation, and long-term growth.

This chapter unpacks the real-world ethics of AI marketing: what's acceptable, what crosses the line, and how to build trust with your audience while still reaping the benefits of AI-driven efficiency.

What AI Can (and Can't) Do Ethically

AI can be incredibly powerful — but not everything it *can* do is aligned with ethical marketing practices. Understanding the difference is the first step in using AI responsibly.

What's Ethically Sound

- **Personalizing based on real user intent** (pages viewed, products browsed)
- **Using AI to reduce bias** when properly trained on diverse data
- **Automating content, emails, and workflows** to enhance customer experience
- **Respecting opt-in and consent** in every touchpoint

What's Questionable (or Flat-Out Risky)

- **Hyper-targeting based on sensitive traits** (e.g., ethnicity, health conditions, or religious affiliations)
- **Using deceptive copy created by AI** that mimics urgency or false scarcity
- **Deploying AI chatbots without clear disclosure** that users are speaking to a bot
- **Collecting data without clear, explicit permission**

Ethical Actions	Risky Actions
Tailoring content based on user behavior	Micro-targeting with sensitive attributes
Anonymizing personal information	Tracking users without consent
Simplifying mundane tasks	Overriding human decision-making
Disclosing AI usage in campaigns	Providing insufficient explanations

Remember: Ethics isn't about what's legal — it's about what builds long-term trust and brand equity.

How to Avoid Biased Targeting or Creepy Automation

AI doesn't create bias — but it can amplify it if left unchecked.

Most AI models learn from historical data, and if that data reflects biased assumptions, the outcomes will too. This can lead to discriminatory ad targeting, tone-deaf personalization, or exclusion of high-potential segments.

How to Keep AI Targeting Fair and Inclusive

- **Audit your data sources**: Ensure your customer data reflects a diverse audience
- **Review AI-generated copy**: Look for tone, assumptions, or phrasing that may alienate or stereotype
- **Avoid "too much" personalization**: Just because you *can* mention someone's recent browsing habits doesn't mean you should
- **Build in feedback loops**: Allow users to correct, opt out, or shape their experience

Real-World Example

A health and wellness brand unintentionally excluded older adults from seeing its ads after using an AI audience tool that over-indexed on fitness influencers. After adjusting inputs and including broader behavior patterns (like sleep concerns and nutrition interests), their reach and conversion among 50+ users surged by 38%.

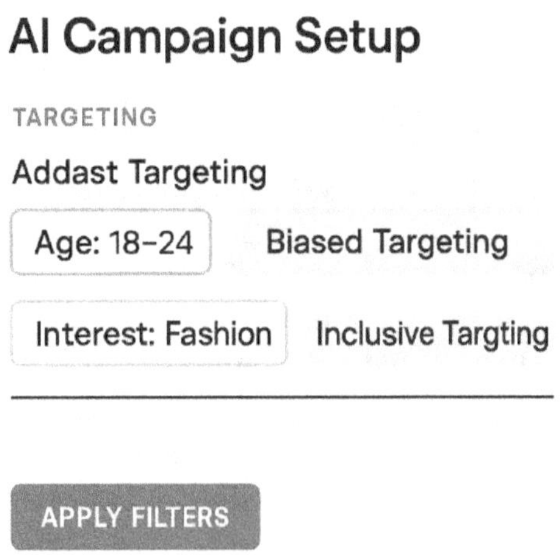

Transparency with Your Customers

Transparency builds trust — especially when automation is involved. Customers want to know:

- **What's being collected**
- **Why it's being used**
- **How they can control it**

SMBs that are clear and honest about their use of AI and data build deeper, longer-lasting customer relationships.

What Good Transparency Looks Like

- A short statement in your emails: *"This email was personalized using your recent site activity."*
- Clear opt-in for AI-driven chat or support: *"You're chatting with our smart assistant. Want a human? Click here."*
- Privacy policies written in **plain English**, not legal jargon
- Visible unsubscribe or data control options in every message

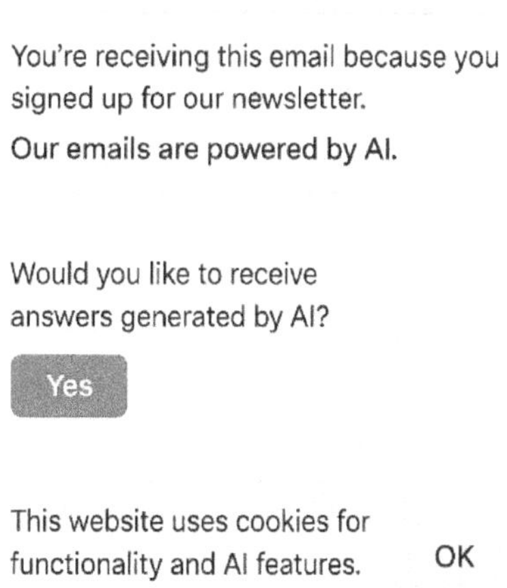

Transparency isn't just polite — it's a business advantage. Customers are more willing to share data with brands that are upfront about how it's used.

Trust-Building Tips in Automated Marketing

Automation doesn't have to feel robotic. In fact, the smartest AI marketing is **invisible to the customer** — it simply creates smoother, more relevant experiences. But trust must be *actively earned* through every interaction.

Practical Trust-Building Tactics

- **Always give users control**: Let them update preferences, pause automations, or choose communication channels
- **Include human elements**: Even automated emails can include your team's name, photo, or personal note
- **Balance personalization with boundaries**: Refer to recent activity, but don't reference private or overly specific behavior
- **Be honest about your intent**: AI should help — not manipulate

Tactical Checklist

- ☐ Review all automation flows for tone and clarity
- ☐ Include plain-language disclosures on key forms and emails
- ☐ Regularly audit targeting logic to spot exclusion or over-targeting
- ☐ Train your team on ethical use of AI — not just how to use the tools

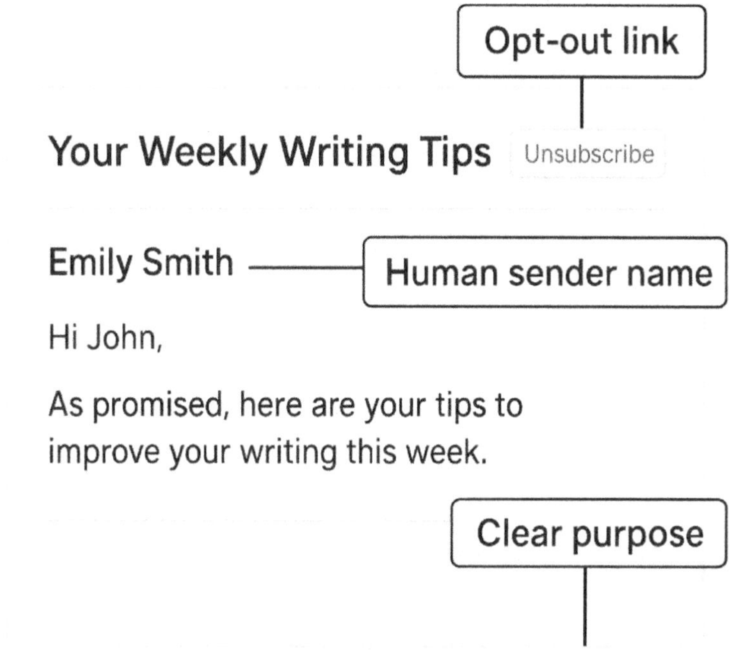

Real-World Example: Earning Trust with AI Transparency

Business Type: Online Learning Platform
Challenge: Low email open rates and rising unsubscribe complaints
Old Approach:

- Personalized emails based on course browsing — without disclosing how
- AI-generated copy with overly aggressive subject lines and urgency tactics

Revised Strategy:

- Added a note in each email: "This email was tailored to your interests in [topic]"
- Shifted tone from "act now" to "based on your goals, we thought this might help"
- Updated privacy page to explain how AI powers recommendations

Outcome:

- 2x improvement in email engagement
- 57% reduction in unsubscribes
- Improved customer sentiment in support tickets

Common Pitfalls to Avoid

- **Over-automating sensitive touchpoints**: Sales or support interactions often require a human
- **Ignoring bias in AI-generated content**: Even well-meaning messaging can alienate if unchecked
- **Hiding AI use**: Customers lose trust when they discover personalization or targeting after the fact
- **Using "dark patterns"**: Manipulative tactics (fake timers, disguised CTAs) damage trust and reputation

Conclusion

AI has incredible power to enhance your marketing — but with power comes responsibility. Ethical, bias-aware, and transparent AI use isn't just about compliance — it's about building a brand that customers can trust, support, and recommend.

For SMBs, this is your edge: showing that you care not just about the click, but about the **customer behind it**.

Next Steps

Review your current use of AI. Are you telling users when and how it's being used? Are you balancing personalization with privacy? Start with one automation — like an email sequence or ad segment — and apply the ethical lens outlined here.

In **Chapter 10: Future-Proof Your Marketing — Scaling with AI**, we'll bring it all together. You'll learn how to turn your AI-powered tactics into a repeatable system that grows with your business — and explore the trends that will shape the next generation of AI marketing.

Chapter 10: Future-Proof Your Marketing — Scaling with AI

Introduction

If there's one lesson from this book, it's this: AI is not just a toolkit for faster marketing — it's a foundation for *smarter* growth. But while most SMBs start with AI in pockets — a smarter email here, a better ad there — the real power comes when you step back and connect the dots.

That's what future-proofing is all about.

To stay competitive in today's landscape (and tomorrow's), you need more than one-off tactics. You need a system. A repeatable, AI-enhanced marketing machine that keeps learning, improving, and scaling — even when you're focused on running the business.

In this final chapter, we'll show you how to go from tactical wins to strategic mastery. We'll walk through how to build a sustainable AI-driven marketing engine, highlight the trends that are reshaping digital marketing, and give you a concrete, checklist-style plan to implement what you've learned — no overwhelm, no fluff.

How to Create a System, Not Just Tactics

Anyone can use AI to run a better campaign. But the most successful SMBs are building **systems** that work across their entire customer journey — powered by AI from first click to final sale (and beyond).

What a System Looks Like

- **Attract** with AI-optimized content, ads, and social media scheduling
- **Engage** with personalized landing pages, email sequences, and chatbots
- **Convert** with predictive lead scoring, dynamic CTAs, and optimized funnels
- **Retain** with smart segmentation, re-engagement flows, and churn prediction

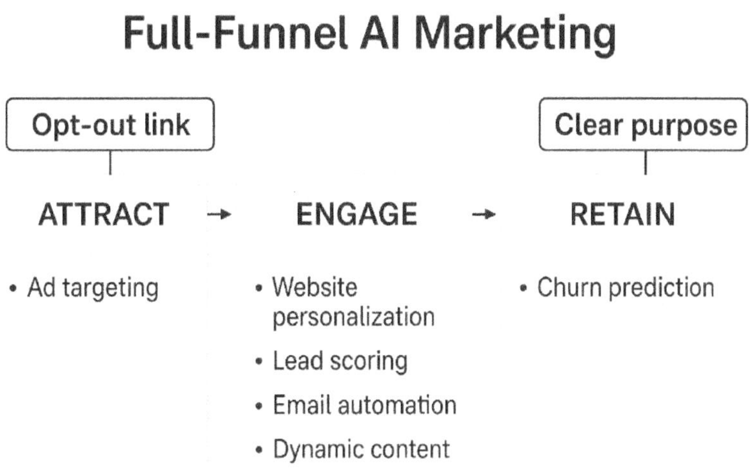

This image illustrates a **Full-Funnel AI Marketing** system, divided into four key phases, each with mapped AI tools:

1. **ATTRACT**
   - Tool: *Ad targeting*
   - Focus: Drawing in potential leads via intelligent ad distribution.
2. **ENGAGE**
   - Tools: *Website personalization, lead scoring, email automation, dynamic content*
   - Focus: Capturing attention and nurturing interest with tailored interactions.
3. **CONVERT** *(not shown but implied between engage → retain)*
   - Typically involves checkout optimization, personalized offers, etc.
4. **RETAIN**
   - Tool: *Churn prediction*
   - Focus: Keeping customers through predictive retention strategies.

The visual emphasizes transparency with side notes like "Opt-out link" and "Clear purpose," reinforcing ethical AI practices throughout the customer journey.

When these components talk to each other, you no longer depend on luck or guesswork. You're working a *repeatable engine* that scales with you.

Building a Repeatable, AI-Enhanced Marketing Machine

Let's translate the big picture into something actionable. What does an AI-powered marketing machine look like on the ground?

5 Building Blocks to Install:

1. **Content Generation Hub**
   - Tools like Jasper, ChatGPT, or Copy.ai for blogs, emails, and posts
   - SEO tools with AI overlays (e.g., SurferSEO)
2. **Ad Automation Engine**
   - Use Meta Ads + Google Performance Max with dynamic creative
   - AI-driven A/B testing and audience optimization
3. **Lead Capture & Nurture Flow**
   - Instapage or Unbounce for personalized landing pages
   - ActiveCampaign or Mailchimp AI for drip campaigns and scoring
4. **Analytics & Prediction Layer**
   - Google Analytics 4 + Piwik PRO for trends and forecasts
   - Looker Studio for visual dashboards
5. **Trust & Transparency Framework**
   - Clear opt-ins, human-friendly disclosures, ethical AI usage
   - Feedback loops to keep content aligned with audience expectations

Result?

You create once, test continuously, and scale automatically — instead of reinventing the wheel every quarter.

What's Coming Next

AI is moving fast — but if you build the right foundation now, you're positioned to adapt, adopt, and accelerate as new capabilities emerge.

Here's what to watch — and prepare for:

Hyper-Personalization

Go beyond first names and basic segments. AI will soon power real-time website personalization based on *live behavior* — not just past data.

- Product recommendations that shift as users scroll
- Real-time chat support based on predictive pain points
- Content that updates mid-session to reflect evolving intent

AI Video Content

Text-based AI is just the start. Tools like Synthesia and Pictory already generate short-form videos with AI-generated narration, animation, and localization.

- Product demos from a script
- Explainers and tutorials for onboarding
- Personalized thank-you videos at scale

Real-Time Intent Signals

Marketing will shift from "hope they're interested" to "know they're ready."

- AI will detect buying signals across channels: email clicks, pricing page visits, ad views
- Tools will alert you the moment a lead is ready for sales — not a day later
- Even B2B firms will benefit from account-level intelligence for timing and messaging

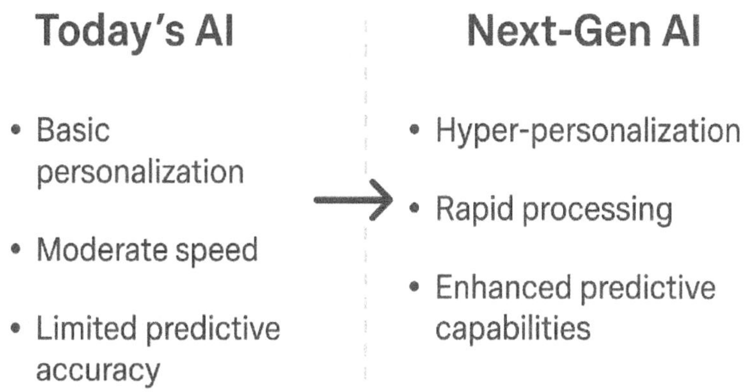

Checklist: Your AI Marketing Starter Plan

To make all of this real — without overwhelm — here's a checklist to begin your AI-powered marketing transformation:

👇 Your First 30-Day Plan

- ☐ **Pick one content task** to automate with AI (e.g., weekly blog or email)
- ☐ **Install one analytics tool** with predictive insights (GA4 or Piwik PRO)
- ☐ **Launch a dynamic ad** using Meta or Google Performance Max
- ☐ **Segment your email list** using AI scoring or tags
- ☐ **Add one AI-powered landing page** using Unbounce or Instapage
- ☐ **Review your data use and opt-ins** for transparency and trust

Scaling Over 90 Days

- ☐ Build a simple, full-funnel system (content → ad → page → email → nurture)
- ☐ Automate re-engagement sequences and churn detection
- ☐ Create dashboards that track performance, not just clicks
- ☐ Identify next-gen tools for video, personalization, or predictive selling

AI Marketing Checklist:
From Tools to Engine

☑ **Define Objectives**
Align AI goals with business strategy
ChatGPT UseMotion Clevop.AI

☑ **Pick Platforms**
Select systems that integrate AI functions
HubSpot ActiveCampaign Zoho

☑ **Enhance Execution**
Automate tasks like ads, emails, and content
Jasper Optimove Copy.ai

☑ **Personalize Experiences**
Use AI to refine messaging and user journeys
Boomtrain Drift CaliberMind

☑ **Optimize Performance**
Apply AI analytics for iterative improvement
Gong.io Writesonic Seventh Sense

Conclusion

You've just completed a full blueprint for using AI to modernize, optimize, and **future-proof** your marketing. From smarter content and personalized campaigns to predictive analytics and automated funnels, AI has shifted the marketing advantage to SMBs who are **willing to act.**

But remember — it's not about chasing every shiny tool. It's about building **a system that scales**. A system powered by insight, trust, and intelligent automation — with you firmly in control.

Whether you're a solopreneur, a growing agency, or a founder ready to take your business to the next level, this is your moment. AI isn't replacing marketers. It's empowering the best ones.

And now — that includes you.

Final Word

Thank you for investing the time to think strategically about your marketing future. If you implement even a fraction of what you've learned here, you'll see the difference — in your visibility, your conversion rates, and your confidence.

You're not just adopting new tools. You're building a smarter, more resilient business.

Let's make your marketing unstoppable.

CHECK YOUR BONUS AT THE END !

Glossary: AI-Driven Marketing for SMBs

This glossary distills the key terms and concepts covered throughout the book. Whether you're a first-time AI user or building a long-term marketing system, use this section as a quick reference to clarify the language behind modern, AI-enhanced marketing.

A/B Testing

A method of comparing two or more versions of a piece of content (such as an email subject line or ad headline) to see which performs better. AI automates and accelerates this process by testing multiple variants simultaneously and adjusting in real time.

AI (Artificial Intelligence)

The use of algorithms and machine learning models to analyze data, recognize patterns, make decisions, and perform tasks that typically require human intelligence. In marketing, AI is used for content creation, audience targeting, ad optimization, personalization, and more.

AI Copywriting Tools

Software like **Jasper**, **ChatGPT**, and **Copy.ai** that use natural language processing (NLP) to generate marketing content, from blog posts to ad headlines and emails, based on prompts and business goals.

Analytics Dashboard

A visual interface that displays marketing performance metrics such as traffic, conversions, engagement, and ROI. AI-enhanced dashboards surface the most relevant insights and often include predictive suggestions.

Audience Segmentation

Dividing your audience into groups based on shared characteristics, behaviors, or preferences. AI improves this process by using real-time behavior, purchase history, and engagement data to build smarter, more dynamic segments.

Automation

The use of software to perform repetitive marketing tasks — such as sending emails, scheduling posts, or qualifying leads — without human intervention. AI-powered automation adds intelligence by adapting based on user behavior.

Behavioral Targeting

Delivering content or offers to users based on their past behavior, such as page visits, purchases, or engagement history. AI enhances behavioral targeting by predicting next steps and personalizing content in real time.

Chatbot

An AI-powered virtual assistant used on websites or messaging apps to interact with customers, answer questions, qualify leads, and route inquiries — often 24/7.

Churn Prediction

An AI capability that forecasts which customers are most likely to stop buying or unsubscribe based on behavioral patterns. Enables timely re-engagement efforts.

Conversion Funnel

The path a customer takes from awareness to action (such as signing up, buying, or booking). AI improves funnels by optimizing each step based on user data and predicting where drop-offs may occur.

CRM (Customer Relationship Management)

A platform used to manage interactions with prospects and customers. AI-enhanced CRMs (e.g., HubSpot, Zoho) include lead scoring, predictive insights, and behavior-triggered automations.

CTA (Call to Action)

A prompt that encourages users to take a specific action, such as "Sign Up," "Buy Now," or "Book a Demo." AI can test different CTAs and optimize placement and language for higher conversion.

Dynamic Content

Content that changes based on the user's profile, behavior, or preferences. AI automates the delivery of personalized headlines, offers, or visuals in emails, ads, and landing pages.

Email Nurture Sequence

A series of automated emails designed to educate and guide leads toward a buying decision. AI personalizes the timing, messaging, and content based on user engagement.

Funnel Mapping

The process of visually outlining your customer journey — from first interaction to final sale. AI tools like Funnelytics track real-time data to improve each funnel stage.

Geo-Targeting

Using a user's geographic location to tailor content, ads, or offers. AI refines this by identifying high-performing regions and adjusting targeting dynamically.

Heatmaps

Visual representations of where users click, scroll, or hover on a web page. AI interprets these maps to optimize design and content placement.

Hyper-Personalization

An advanced form of personalization that uses AI to deliver real-time, one-to-one content based on live behavior, preferences, and context.

Intent Signals

Behaviors that indicate a customer is close to taking action, such as viewing pricing pages or downloading a lead magnet. AI detects and acts on these signals to time outreach effectively.

Landing Page

A standalone web page focused on a single goal — like capturing leads or promoting a product. AI tools (Unbounce, Instapage) can optimize design and personalize content based on visitor behavior.

Lead Scoring

The process of ranking prospects based on how likely they are to convert. AI lead scoring models analyze behavior and demographics to automatically prioritize high-quality leads.

Lookalike Audience

A group of users who resemble your existing customers in behavior, interests, and demographics. AI uses data to create these audiences for ad targeting on platforms like Facebook and Google.

Marketing Automation

Technology that streamlines and automates repetitive marketing tasks across channels. When powered by AI, automation becomes responsive and predictive.

Performance Max Campaigns (Google)

A type of AI-driven ad campaign that automatically runs across Google's full network — Search, Display, YouTube, Gmail, and Maps — optimizing creative and targeting for results.

Predictive Analytics

A technique that uses historical data, behavior, and AI modeling to forecast future actions — such as which users are likely to convert, churn, or engage.

Real-Time Personalization

The ability to adapt content, recommendations, or offers instantly based on user activity. AI makes this possible at scale, across websites, emails, and ads.

Re-Engagement Flow

A sequence of communications triggered when a lead or customer becomes inactive. AI identifies disengagement patterns and recommends the best time, message, and offer to re-capture interest.

Retargeting

Serving ads to people who have previously interacted with your website or brand. AI enhances this by customizing ad content to reflect user behavior and likelihood to convert.

Smart Scheduling

Using AI to determine the best time to publish content or send emails for maximum engagement based on user patterns and platform data.

Social Listening

Monitoring social platforms for mentions of your brand, competitors, or key topics. AI tools add sentiment analysis and trend detection to surface opportunities and risks.

Transparency (AI Use)

Disclosing to customers when AI is being used — such as in chatbots, recommendations, or personalized content — to build trust and comply with ethical standards.

Bonus – FREE eBook Version

Want the full-color PDF version of this book?
Simply email me at **ericl@acrasolution.com** with a **screenshot of your Amazon purchase and positive review**, and I'll gladly send you your personal copy.

Thank you for taking the time to read this eBook.

Your support means more than you know. **By purchasing this book, you're directly contributing to the creation of more high-quality, practical resources** for business owners, IT leaders, and everyday professionals navigating the complex world of cybersecurity. It's because of readers like you that I can continue researching, writing, and delivering tools that make a real difference.

Whether you leave a positive review, recommend this book to a colleague, or simply apply what you've learned — **you're helping grow a stronger, safer business community. And for that, I sincerely thank you.**

At **AcraSolution**, we're committed to providing both premium services and a wide range of **free, actionable tools**. Our growing library includes documentation, articles, and step-by-step guides — designed to bring you immediate value, no strings attached.

If you need additional guidance or support, don't hesitate to visit our website www.acrasolution.com or reach out directly.

Together, we can build a more secure future.

– Eric LeBouthillier
Author & Cybersecurity Strategist

www.ingramcontent.com/pod-product-compliance
Lightning Source LLC
LaVergne TN
LVHW022116200926
848481LV00003B/1178
* 9 7 8 1 0 6 9 6 4 3 7 9 7 *